THE DAILY 180°

Inspirational Perspectives and Reflections for Educators

J.D. DURDEN

Copyright © 2024
Published by Education Renovation, LLC.
J.D. Durden
The Daily 180°
Inspirational Perspectives and Reflections for Educators
All rights reserved.

J.D. Durden

Printed Worldwide
First Printing 2024
First Edition 2024

10 9 8 7 6 5 4 3 2 1

For permission requests, contact jd@jddurden.com

For more information about booking and bulk purchases, please connect at www.jddurden.com

Disclaimer
The information in this book is intended for educational coaching only. It is not for diagnosis, prescription, or treatment of any disorder and should not replace consultation with healthcare professionals.

THE DAILY 180°

DEDICATION

To all educators in the world. Without education, we have no foundation to build upon.

Thank you for being society's foundation.

IN MEMORY OF CALEB G.

You were a sensitive yet feisty educator. You consistently
ensured that students knew their value and were their best
selves. You stood up for them and believed in our future.
Thank you for sharing your many gifts with adults and
youth and making us all better. Thank you for your
wholehearted service. Our future is better because of you.
Your legacy lives on.

PREFACE

Several years ago, I conducted case study research on teachers' morale levels and their intention to stay in education or not. I had clear indications that our already established teacher shortage problem would soon worsen. I needed to know how much.

After the research was concluded, the data showed that more than fifty percent of teachers were actively thinking of ways to get out of education. I started working harder from the inside of buildings rather than trying to change the outer layers of our educational system, realizing that might be the only thing we can control these days.

By choice, I have made decisions not to go into educational administration positions for many reasons. I am, however, a teacher leader who hyper-observes, studies educational environments, and collects data while developing and championing organizational culture-shifting plans and initiatives across schools and districts.

With the new knowledge of how teachers were feeling and how I felt, I spent an entire contracted school year—one hundred eighty days—writing my perspective on real-life happenings around me at work. *The Daily 180°* writings and reflections in this book are thoughts and questions I wrote each morning before my days started. Realizing that shifting my mindset, sometimes 180 degrees, is a guaranteed controllable, this practice kept me focused on the necessary work in education. I was writing primarily for myself, journaling, finding new perspectives, and purposely reminding myself each day of why I keep showing up. By day ninety of writing and self-reflecting, I knew I was writing for everyone in education because I could see you all in my thoughts. We are all in this together, and I know our stories are not that different. What is different in your book from what I wrote for myself is that I left space each day for your reflections.

I hope you grow in more ways than just professionally as you self-reflect and find new and inspired perspectives over the next one hundred eighty days. On days when your perspective needs to shift 180 degrees, I hope you welcome the turnaround and move through your day with an open heart and mind.

Please read a daily inspirational message with a relative self-reflection prompt attached. As you move through the days, you will notice the following key concepts intertwined throughout the book.

- Influence
- Reality
- Relationships
- Resilience
- Reflection
- Retention
- Mindfulness
- Kindness
- Leadership
- Accountability
- Honesty
- Emotional Intelligence
- Social Intelligence
- Cultural Intelligence
- Empathy
- Optimism
- Change
- Expectation
- Failure
- Success
- Internal Wealth

DAY ONE

School starts today, a big deal to us and an even bigger deal to our youth. You have 179 contracted days after this—give or take a few.

Educators, you are the bedrock of our society. Your resilience, dedication, and unwavering commitment to your students make our communities thrive. As you embark on this new school year, may you always remember the profound impact you have on the lives of those around you. We are grateful for your service and the difference you make every single day.

Good luck, and know that approximately eighty-five million teachers feel like you do today!

What are three goals that you wish to accomplish today?

DAY TWO

Day one can wipe us out and feel like one week all in one day, so remember, taking naps is essential for brain power. As tired as you may feel today, I'm sure you are reminded of *why* you do this job. We are a privileged group of humans who get to live through the eyes of our youth. At every age and stage, we get to love, be loved, and be an influence on so many levels.

With education as our vehicle, we hold endless influence. On the road of life, we may never know the distance our influence may travel.

What positive influence can you have on your students today?

DAY THREE

The students sitting in front of you today are our future. They will be taking over when we retire and move on. They are the change makers, the lawmakers, the love, the hate, the kindness, and the brains of what our world will be like for generations to come. Our responsibility is to serve their interests and shape and guide them to the best of our ability. We hold a vital opportunity to influence the future positively through our students. We must be mindful and careful with this opportunity.

As the students in front of us form their characteristics and contribution to this world, what will you add to their experience as their teacher?

Day Four

As much as we are privileged to share space with our youth, our youth are lucky to share space with you. As intentional and meaningful educators, we can make or break a student's day, week, and year. If we are constantly inspiring, despite our demands, our youth will prosper . . . and so will we. I dare you to remain dedicated to creative teaching with heart. In the end, that is your legacy.

Because you will be a core memory for many students, what do you want your legacy to be when students remember you?

Day Five

Take time for yourself today and tonight. If you can close your eyes at lunch, do so. Breathe in and breathe out. Find some gratitude in this long first week. Consider activities like a short walk, listening to calming music, or practicing mindfulness. Enter into your afternoon with the intention to leave smiles with those around you. You never know what kids deal with at home.

Tonight, nourish your tired body with a well-balanced dinner. Remember, your well-being is crucial to your ability to educate and care for others. Take time to rest and rejuvenate, making mindful choices for your time and mind. Remember, it's not selfish to prioritize self-care. We value you, and our future depends on your well-being.

What is your plan for tonight and the weekend? Try to implement this thought process each weekend of the school year.

DAY SIX

Safety is the priority in teaching. If our youth do not feel safe, then learning cannot happen. The same thing applies to adults in education. If we do not feel safe, we cannot do our jobs to the best of our ability. The beauty of being an adult is that we can control our environments for the most part.

Every single person is someone else's person. Whether you are a spouse, a parent, a grandparent, a sibling, or an aunt or uncle to someone, we should take care of each other like they were our child, sibling, nephew, or grandchild. This means we all have reasons to take care of each other.

As educators, we are responsible for finding ways for ourselves and our students to feel safe, comfortable, loved, and celebrated every day. Each of us plays a crucial role in this, and our contributions are invaluable to the well-being of our educational communities and beyond.

What are the small and big ways you create a safe
environment for yourself and others?

DAY SEVEN

Maybe day seven feels like day seventeen or seventy because our job requires full-force energy 100% of the time.

Feeling valued is an integral part of our success, individually and collectively. Unfortunately, it's a rarity to feel valued in our education system. So, we have to take care of the value system ourselves.

Find humans around you who know how to express gratitude rather than mostly complaining. Spend time around those who value your expertise and all you offer.

Remember to reflect gratitude, value, and positivity; we must give it out first.

In what ways can you attract value and positivity? How can you shift your thinking to find the beauty in where you are each day?

_____

_____

_____

_____

_____

_____

_____

_____

_____

_____

_____

_____

_____

_____

_____

_____

_____

_____

DAY EIGHT

We live in a world where "more" is better. Our educational
system has become the same in this regard—more of this
and that and constant changes: better test scores and results,
better performance evaluations. The problem is that we have
little support to get there in a healthy way. What if we
shifted the "more" mindset to serve us better as we move
through the demands on educators?

More self-love.

More outward love.

More understanding.

More kindness.

More grace.

More lifting others up.

More walking.

More healthy meals.

More drinking water.

More of being in the moment.

. . .

What can you do "more" this year to balance your life and create more happiness?

DAY NINE

Educators are directly responsible for how we make those around us feel. We are human. Life is tough. While on this rollercoaster of life, how do we ensure that our emotional state is not projected onto others? A daily self-reflection can reveal solutions if we are honest with ourselves. One of our significant responsibilities within humanity is to prevent possible emotional damage to others because of our own issues. We often get in cycles of thinking everything bad that is happening is because of others, but many times . . . it is us. We might be angry that our son is failing English, so we write up the boy who disrupted class once. That's not fair to him, and the adult is responsible.

Administering self-reflection is one of the most professional action steps we can control.

Does your personal life influence how you interact and react to events professionally?

Does your job influence your interactions at home?

_____

_____

_____

_____

_____

_____

_____

_____

_____

_____

_____

_____

_____

_____

_____

_____

Day Ten

Today, you should celebrate *you* for all you give, take on, and balance in the name of education and helping our youth.

Take a moment, close your eyes, and take a deep breath. Pat yourself on your heart (because this is where you live) and thank yourself.

Go ahead; it's hard to give ourselves credit sometimes, but this is a safe place to express gratitude for your*self*.

This is a perfect page to jot down as much gratitude to yourself as possible.

Thank you for waking up! taking steps forward and educating our youth!!!

DAY ELEVEN

You showed up! Look at you! You showed up for a new start, a new perspective, and maybe . . . just maybe, a new outcome.

However, just showing up is sometimes not good enough. Once we show up, what do we do with the time we're given?

Showing up as your best self is a much better option than giving up.

What do the best show-up moments look like for you?

DAY TWELVE

Gossip is the poison that kills so many relationships. Why do we do it? What is the ultimate purpose? Having a true friend you can confide in and share concerns with is one thing. It's an entirely different thing to sit around humans we don't know and trust them with information that is usually not ours to share. This is toxic behavior that contributes to your overall environment.

We can do better. If we expect our youth not to gossip and hurt others, we should also rise to that expectation.

Be the adult who is well respected because you don't spread information that's not yours. Be the adult who has boundaries and is emotionally intelligent. This is the only way others can genuinely trust you.

What boundaries will you set for yourself to rise above gossip and negativity?

DAY THIRTEEN

We cannot assume that we automatically deserve respect as adults. To truly earn respect, we must first show it to other humans, regardless of age.

Respect is earned, especially with our youth. They see right through us. Our students know when we are being authentic or not. They do not respect us automatically because we think they should. Today's generation has independence and decides much of their lives for themselves, and that's okay. Should they have respect for elders like we were taught? Yes, if we deserve it. Some adults who hurt others don't deserve respect.

If you are struggling with a student because you feel a lack of respect, talk to that student. Sometimes, that is all it takes for them to feel seen.

Do you have a student or adult you feel disrespects you?
After self-reflection, how can you change the dynamics of
interactions?

_____

_____

_____

_____

_____

_____

_____

_____

_____

_____

_____

_____

_____

_____

_____

_____

DAY FOURTEEN

It's a choice to be where we are at this moment. Some may not think it's a choice because of family responsibilities, bills, insurance, etc. But in the end, it is our choice. If we like where we choose to be, then that's great! If we hate where we are or feel like our soul is dying, choose something else.

We cannot blame others for what we choose to do with our lives each day. If we are unhappy where we are, we must be aware of how we treat others when we feel dissatisfied. No one deserves to get our worst (especially kids) when we have our own issues to work out.

If you are happy where you are, share why.

If you are unhappy where you are, share why and what you
need to do to make a change.

Are others around you getting less than your best?

DAY FIFTEEN

How can we use our skills and talents to make an actual difference? Some of us are natural leaders. Some of us want to change the world. Some of us want to make our classrooms the best they can be. Some of us like to ensure safety on all levels. Some of us love to make connections. Whatever our "thing" is that we do well, that's the area where we give our all.

Once we give our all authentically, making a difference is inevitable. Creating change and culture shifts happens when we all show up sharing our unique skills and talents.

What skills and talents do you bring to work? How do your
skills and talents improve your environment?

_____

_____

_____

_____

_____

_____

_____

_____

_____

_____

_____

_____

_____

_____

_____

_____

DAY SIXTEEN

It sometimes feels like we are all being asked to be the same in education: use the same curriculum, do the same things at the same pace, and not veer too far from the group's way of doing things.

Do we need to deliver what we teach in the same way? No.

Be creative. It sets you apart from others and gives our students a diverse educational experience.

In what ways are you a unique educator for those around you?

DAY SEVENTEEN

No is the best two-letter power word. In some cases, it's your superpower. So often, we say yes because it feels awkward and unkind to say no. When we say yes to everything, we wear ourselves thin by overcommitting. We might not correctly serve the yes because we can't give our all. Teaching is all-consuming as it is, and adding additional yes commitments can ignite unneeded anxiety. If we say no more often and save the yes for the right moments, more success will follow, and we will have a healthier mentality. If we say no more often, we can focus more on what matters the most.

Sometimes, what matters the most is outside of work, and that's okay.

What matters the most to you? How can you balance your
yes and no commitments?

_____

_____

_____

_____

_____

_____

_____

_____

_____

_____

_____

_____

_____

_____

_____

_____

_____

DAY EIGHTEEN

We grow where we are allowed to grow, where the soil is rich, and where people support us and give us opportunities with consistent kudos. We grow where we can be ourselves as humans and educators. We grow where we feel valued.

Genuine self-reflection happens when we may not feel valued. That's when we get honest about what *is* and what *is not* helping us grow and supporting us in being the best we can be.

How is your environment serving your growth? Or not?

Day Nineteen

Every single day can be good if we demand it. I'm not saying it's all butterflies and rainbows, but we can respond to almost everything positively and get the most out of our days. Believe it or not, we are in control.

We may not have control over many things outside of ourselves, but our power lies in how we respond to those things we cannot control. In fact, we can change the environment in which we react to situations. Adults and students around us watch, mimic, and take notes on how we respond to life. We all have to do our part to create the environments we want.

How are you responding to life lately? How can you change
your reactions to create a more positive environment?

DAY TWENTY

Not only are we in charge of how our days go, but we are also responsible for those around us. How can we lift them up? How can we support them? How can we make them smile and laugh? How can we be a grounding force? Only you know how to do these things, which requires some self-reflection.

Every negative word, action, or energy we release into the world is a missed opportunity to better the world around us.

What are your actions and language telling others?

DAY TWENTY-ONE

There are no bad kids.

Let me say that again.

There are no bad kids.

That one student who may drive you crazy. That one kid who brings out the worst in you. That one kid has reasons. Try to let them bring out the best in you. Give them more than a few chances.

There are no bad kids.

All humans are born with unconditional love and acceptance. We want to be loved; no matter how pain in life changes us, we still want that love.

We get the opportunity to show others love and acceptance, show them that there is good in the world, and show them that there are high expectations because we believe in them. We get to model boundaries so they know their limits. We all get to show up for these kids and create balance in our environments.

How are you showing love with boundaries to create the most balance in your life—professionally and personally?

_____

_____

_____

_____

_____

_____

_____

_____

_____

_____

_____

_____

_____

_____

_____

_____

_____

_____

DAY TWENTY-TWO

It's not always what we do for a living, but how we make
others feel around us along the way.

We may not get paid the most monetarily, but we do make
a difference. We are making personal investments in our
collective future. Should we get paid more? Yes. Let's
continue to let that be known. But, for now, on this day,
you get to change someone's outlook on life. You get to
grow a brain. You get to be a consistent adult in someone's
life. You get to be the smiling face that gives a kid a reason
to show up to school. You even get to save lives.

You are a big deal.

What is your plan to make someone's day today?

DAY TWENTY-THREE

We have many gifts, but our most significant gift is to love and see others—*all* others.

Care without judgment. Equal treatment. Consistent respect. Controlled biases.

Imagine our schools and world if we could all implement these actions.

To be a good educator, these actions matter. The kids can pick up on mistreatment, judgment, or bias and know if we have teacher favorites in the room. Equal treatment is what they deserve, and you are the person to follow through with these actions. Thank goodness you are where you are right now and doing what you do best. We are human, we make mistakes, and some of these actions are hard to produce sometimes. But we can always get back on track for the sake of how each heart feels around us. No one should ever feel "less than."

What can you do today? Be aware of how you show love
without judgment, equal treatment, consistent respect, and
controlled biases.

DAY TWENTY-FOUR

No, our jobs are not all rainbows and butterflies, and yes, we go home exhausted many days. Still, we have the power within us to make today and every day turn out exactly how we want.

At school and home.

How can you shift the energy around you to be positive and healthy at any given moment of the day?

DAY TWENTY-FIVE

Undoubtedly, finding a balance between our home and work life isn't easy. If we are on point at home, we often feel off-kilter at work. If we are rocking things at work, there is no doubt that our home life may suffer somehow. No one can tell us how to find our perfect balance; we can only keep trying to find what works best. We owe it to ourselves and those we love. This may mean letting go of some things to find that perfect-ish balance for your life.

Keep trying! You will get there, and some days will be better than others.

What can you rearrange, let go of, or change to gain more balance between work and home?

DAY TWENTY-SIX

Fear can paralyze us. What are we fearful of? Who is making us feel fear? Has someone or something created fear-based thinking that you hold on to?

Remember, we are the only people who can cancel out fear and replace it with positive emotions. If the fear is deeply ingrained, this may take some time, but you have the upper hand. I dare you to use your power to feel free.

What are some ways you may be living fearfully? How can you shift your emotions?

_____

_____

_____

_____

_____

_____

_____

_____

_____

_____

_____

_____

_____

_____

_____

_____

DAY TWENTY-SEVEN

Don't be confused; caution is not necessarily fear. Caution is essential, especially in education. We have much to be careful about for our youth and want to ensure they are cared for appropriately. Still, we cannot allow our caution to turn into fear.

Be brave! Step out and change what you want to change. Ask the tough questions. Be the leader you are meant to be.

What can be so bad on the other side of being brave and standing up for what is right for our youth?

DAY TWENTY-EIGHT

Starting over.

Any child or adult can choose to start over at any time, and
we can also choose to let others start over. We *should* give
our youth opportunities to start over.

Their missteps are not personal, and holding grudges does
not benefit anyone. Our youth need restarts almost daily,
and it's within our power to help them feel supported. We
can make or break a life by showing them grace and
forgiveness and allowing safe spaces where they can mess up
and start over.

Where can you start over today? What person in your life deserves a space to start over?

_____

_____

_____

_____

_____

_____

_____

_____

_____

_____

_____

_____

_____

_____

_____

_____

DAY TWENTY-NINE

"Fake it 'til you make it" is real sometimes. Some days are more challenging than others, and we are human. No matter how seasoned we are, pretending to be present, happy, or on point is a natural occurrence that gets us through some days.

The beautiful part about "faking" is that, eventually, we will feel better. We can convince ourselves that life is better than it might appear. This positive psychology can turn your day, week, or year around. To bring that concept to the next level, you might even make someone else's day by forcing yourself to simply . . . smile.

Today, show your fantastic smile. Our world needs it!

How are you feeling today? Can you dig deep to show
happiness, even if it's not how you feel?

DAY THIRTY

A wise person and teacher coached her classes on the lesson of integrity. British writer C. S. Lewis said, "Integrity is doing the right thing, even when no one is watching."

Integrity runs deep in who we are and who we are not, and people notice if we have it or not from miles away. If we do what we say we are doing, live authentically, and behave consistently even when no one is looking, we can live more of a guilt-free life.

We can trust ourselves, and others can trust us.

While at work, how are we choosing to spend our time while no one is looking? Are we doing what we say we are doing?

DAY THIRTY-ONE

Create the space you need not only to survive but eventually to thrive. To thrive means to get out of the old and make some changes; it requires taking care of the small things first.

Start by doing the little things that make you happy. Buy some bamboo plants, brush your teeth after lunch, bring in your favorite chocolates, or write a letter or note to yourself or someone you notice doing great things around you. Thank someone for what they might give to you each day; they probably have no idea they are helping you.

Start something new in your daily routine, like taking a gratitude stroll around the school or building. Meditate over lunch. Sleep more . . . sleep less. Do you! Do the things that make you tick and start the thriving process. Only you have the power—and the power you have is extraordinary.

Where can you make some minor changes to shift from surviving to thriving? If you feel you are already thriving, what changes can you make to thrive more?

DAY THIRTY-TWO

Value is underrepresented in education. We know this. Some leaders effectively create valued environments, while others don't consider the term "value" at all. In a service industry like education, it is often assumed that we all have what it takes to create value for ourselves. But our leadership is required to start the process top-down. Since leaders are human too, they may forget or get too busy, and although this is not an excuse, perhaps it is up to us to create the environment of value we want.

In fact, it is our responsibility to create the culture of value that we want. We cannot depend on someone else to make magic happen. Waiting around for the perfect leader to swoop in and shift everything is not something we have to wait for. Each of us can create the valued system that we want to experience. We do this through positive mindsets, communication, teamwork, gratitude, and smiles.

A leader doesn't create culture; *we* create culture. Complaining is an easy path that leads nowhere. Rising above the complaining and taking action ourselves is the change-maker path.

How can you lead by example and show more value to yourself, your team, your administration, and your students?

_____

_____

_____

_____

_____

_____

_____

_____

_____

_____

_____

_____

_____

_____

_____

_____

Day Thirty-Three

When we forget *why* we are here or can't see a picture through all of the scribbles, we need to look inward. Don't stop at the surface; go further into who you are and try to remember why you signed a contract to teach in the first place. What was your feeling? What did you tell yourself on that day? Were you excited about your journey to give back to others? To change lives?

Life can sometimes suppress our original feelings of why we are here. Knowing when to move on and do something else is admirable, but pause long enough to evaluate your deeper reasoning about whether you should stay or go.

Good luck on this journey.

How did you feel when you signed your 180-day contract to teach, lead, and serve in education?

Do you still feel any of these same feelings?

DAY THIRTY-FOUR

Excellence is not a chore.

Excellence should come quickly and easily the more we practice it. When we are consistent in our work, even when things get hard, the mindset of excellence becomes our norm. Those around us can see and feel our excellence and notice our strength and consistency. Having an excellent work ethic inspires trust within our teams.

Our levels of excellence can also shift daily depending on life's theatrics. But we still put forth the efforts not as a chore but as an opportunity to reach places we couldn't if we gave up when things got too hard.

Excellence is not perfection but the pursuit of greatness.

How's the mindset of excellence going for you these days?

DAY THIRTY-FIVE

If we honestly look into the eyes of the youth before us, we will see their soul. They deal with so much and manage a different world than how we grew up. I always say that comparing the experiences of today's youth with ours is like comparing gas prices from then to now . . . we can't. Too much has changed. We have evolved in remarkable ways.

However, one thing that remains the same generation after generation is how we should treat others. Youth today are humans with hearts, like us, trying to live the best they can with whatever life has given them. They are not less than, not a problem, not what's wrong with the world. With everything they take in from the world, they are what's good and right: deserving of our respect, time, and energy.

They are **our** future.

How can we show the youth in front of us that they deserve
our best?

DAY THIRTY-SIX

Can we think outside the box for a moment? Consider what's not working and how we can improve. How can you or your team fix things or, at the very least, make them better by trying something different?

Life demands innovative thinking to find real solutions, and education is in dire need of such thinking. The only constant in life is change, and life evolves too rapidly for us to continue doing things the same way as in the past.

In our educational system, we want innovation but are not given the resources to innovate. So, like any great inventor, we use our minds as our greatest resource.

We figure out how to move our educational mindsets into *a new day* rather than lingering *back in the day*.

What are some areas where you can think outside the box and improve on areas where you or your team might feel stuck?

_____

_____

_____

_____

_____

_____

_____

_____

_____

_____

_____

_____

_____

_____

_____

_____

_____

_____

DAY THIRTY-SEVEN

If we were to fast-forward to the end of our lives, the only thing that would matter is . . .

How we were loved and how we loved.

Why wait until the end of our lives to give and receive love the way we want? We need all the love we can get, and your love changes lives.

The reality is that test scores and grades matter less than how we connect, teach, and create spaces where everyone belongs. Test scores, ranking, and grades are a small part of our work, but creating these spaces of belonging will support the logistical parts of academic profiles.

What are some ways in which you create spaces where everyone feels that they belong and are loved?

DAY THIRTY-EIGHT

Do you let the opinions of other adults around you steal your joy? I think we all do to some degree. If we are good humans to others, then we can't worry about judgments that may steal our joy. That's their issue, and it probably has nothing to do with us. Let them dwell on the unhappiness they create when judgment appears while you continue to be your best.

The golden rule never gets old. We should treat others the exact way we want to be treated. This practice leads to less drama, and we all should wish for less drama because we have better things to do with our time.

How can you retain your joy amid any judgment around you?

_____
_____
_____
_____
_____
_____
_____
_____
_____
_____
_____
_____
_____
_____
_____
_____
_____

DAY THIRTY-NINE

Whatever behavior and character traits we expect from our students are precisely what we should expect of ourselves as adults.

Kindness

Fairness

Nice Words

Good tone

Acceptance

. . .

What other behaviors and character traits should we expect
from ourselves and the adults around us?

DAY FORTY

GO PLAY!

Create time for yourself to not think about work. Call a friend or a family member, or enjoy your solitude. We are responsible for creating spaces for ourselves to enjoy life to the fullest. No one is going to do it for us.

What activities do you enjoy that you have been unable to do lately? How can you invite them back into your life?

_____

_____

_____

_____

_____

_____

_____

_____

_____

_____

_____

_____

_____

_____

_____

_____

_____

_____

DAY FORTY-ONE

"Intelligence plus character; that is the goal of true education."

Martin Luther King

I dare you to look beyond numbers, data, and grades. Look at the characters before you. Look at the opportunities you have to assist in building character in the students before you and the adults around you. The data will improve alongside character development. We are constantly influencing our environments, and it's our job to show up with our own best character to bring out the best in each other.

What are the characteristics you bring to work every single day? How can you assist others in building their character?

DAY FORTY-TWO

While some of us do not like change, some of us welcome change. In shift moments, we often do not understand or fight against the shift because we need things to remain comfortable.

The truth is, in every change cycle, there is an opportunity for growth individually and collectively. We cannot stay the same as things around us change. It's impossible. So, in the end, while we have less control when things are shifting, we can control how we respond, react, and receive change.

What areas of your life are changing? How can you respond
positively to these changes?

_____

_____

_____

_____

_____

_____

_____

_____

_____

_____

_____

_____

_____

_____

_____

_____

_____

_____

Day Forty-Three

When a group gossips or talks about others behind their backs, we should avoid that negative energy and walk away. Finding our independence in navigating social behavior in our workplace is essential.

It is suggested that humans who are missing something, insecure, or unhappy in their own lives are the ones who gossip, spread lies, and create toxic environments for others, possibly not evolving or developing much beyond high school behavior patterns.

It is in our control to be better than this type of behavior. It's our responsibility to be adults. We can all lead by example by not feeding into the energy of groups that undermine others. Remaining associated with these types of groups is sometimes the easy choice. Walking away is a strength move for yourself and others around you.

How can you move forward in authenticity? How can you be a leader who supports other humans in your environment rather than talking negatively about them?

DAY FORTY-FOUR

When we are humble in *why* we are here for our students, our egos do not get in the way of progression overall. Being humble reduces complaining and barriers that keep us from doing our best. The act of humble living is a proactive approach to being our best selves, best teammates, and best leaders. However, humility does not mean we settle for less or stop fighting for what is right. It doesn't mean we let others run over us or that we give of ourselves freely. When it comes to living a humble life, we must also have healthy boundaries. A successful recipe that enhances and supports being confidently humble

is a dash of:

Spicy

Sweet

Sour

Bold

Salty

What are ways you are confidently humble?

DAY FORTY-FIVE

Although humility is essential, we must also strike a balance between activating strategic risk-taking, advocating for what is right, accepting kudos, and remaining humble along the way. Sometimes, being brave in activism or doing what's right might not look like humility.

That's okay.

There are ways to advocate for what is right by being respectful and mindful as we move through situations. One way is to listen and hear all sides before we take action on how we communicate. There's always a suitable time and place to implement a big idea, change, or do the right thing, and it is usually more successful when we can work with others around us.

Being humble can also include being fierce.

What is "humble advocacy" to you?

DAY FORTY-SIX

Do you know your employer's mission statement? Do you know what it says and what you are representing? If not, look it up and carefully read the words that form the framework for your organization's mission.

After reading it, consider what it means and how it might be similar to or different from your experience. There's always work to be done, and a mission statement should include ongoing goals. Take the words to heart and consider the following questions for your profession.

Do you feel that you represent your organization's mission statement? Do you hold the same values? If not, what is different?

DAY FORTY-SEVEN

It is important to have mental health days, whether taking a day off or taking time on weekends for yourself or with family. We need to breathe, look inward, and regain perspective. Sometimes, we must look at things from another angle to see them for their worth.

You deserve these mental health days; those around you will appreciate and benefit from your self-love moments.

Consider taking a day off for your mental health. What does that look like, and when would be a good time for it?

DAY FORTY-EIGHT

We can't! No matter how hard we try, we cannot walk in someone else's shoes.

But we can practice empathy, compassion, and understanding. We don't have to walk in someone's shoes to understand others better or to have more patience and love as we coexist.

We never truly know what someone is feeling or going through, so our gift to others is to be kind and, at the very least, try to see things from their perspective.

Is there someone you know right now who is going through something you don't quite understand? How can you show up for that person even if you can't relate entirely to their circumstances?

DAY FORTY-NINE

Let's talk finances.

Living on a teacher's salary for your entire adult life is tough. Despite teaching being the most important job in the world, millions of families live paycheck to paycheck, working extra jobs to make ends meet.

Indeed, the only way to live off of a teacher's salary is to live within our means and have zero or very low debt. But this is not always possible if we have to support others. Teachers' kids may feel privileged by who they know in schools, but they sure get told "no" more often than not for things they want at home. We can't afford all that our kids want.

Financial health is just as important as anything we balance in life, and it can happen. Economic freedom is possible. It takes time, but it's worth the time it takes to breathe a little easier.

How can you examine your finances and find a better balance? How might you move toward financial freedom?

Day Fifty

Continuing the financial health discussion is just a reminder that this is another area where we can create more breathing space. Because of the demands we hold at work and all of the responsibilities at home, we can make all of it ten times harder when our finances, or lack thereof, are taking our oxygen.

Taking care of our emotional, physical, mental, ethical, and financial well-being will help us elevate in life.

Why does it feel hard to face this part of your life head-on? Be honest and look at where you think you can make some breakthroughs.

DAY FIFTY-ONE

It is not always easy to bring our best each day. But when we do, we inspire others to do the same, including students and adults.

We can influence how others act, react, respond, and exist around us. When we consistently bring our best—consistency is the key here—it is hard for others to be negative. Some people thrive off of negativity, and that's a choice. The one thing you have control of is you, and if you bring your best, at least your outlook will be bright—consistently.

Are you showing up each day giving your best self? If so, how? If not, how can you shift into this mindset and action? Is there a person around you who interferes with you bringing your best?

DAY FIFTY-TWO

Being responsible for other humans all day is draining and exhausting, but remember your influence. If we stay in a survival mindset, we can't thrive. This is a choice. First, it's a mental choice to decide we will thrive, and second, it's an action choice. We can act on moving into a thriving mindset by changing behaviors, habits, language, and attitudes. Getting there might take some time, but the more we practice a flourishing mindset, the more permanent it will become.

Our influence is vast. We can make or break a kid's day, week, or year. We have the power to change lives. So, in exhaustion, let's influence with our best gifts because our influence is endless. That's what we signed up to do. It's why we still do what we do—the most important job in the world.

Are you in a survival mindset or a thriving mindset? What changes in behaviors, habits, language, and attitudes must you make to shift from survival to thriving?

DAY FIFTY-THREE

Today during lunch, if only for a moment . . . stop. Stop and eat—actually taste the food. Stop and breathe—actually feel your lungs filling up. Stop and think on your own. Listen to a song. Take a lap outside. Meditate. Renew.

We have a work ethic in education that says, "We can't take a break." A perfect example of how we don't stop is that teachers have superhuman bladders because we usually have a few minutes daily to use the bathroom.

Not healthy!

Let's make it a point to take breaks when possible, even if that's only for our short lunch break. This is a conscious choice to take care of *you*. It might be taking care of you in a small way, but these small ways add up.

What changes can you make during your lunch break to renew *you* each day?

DAY FIFTY-FOUR

Right now, you might be thinking, *how can I do this? How can I finish out the year?*

Please remember that you are valued. You are who we need in our schools to support our futures. Even when it does not feel like the adults around you value you, the youth we serve love and value you. They know your worth, talents, and gifts.

If you hate what you are doing, get out. It's that simple. We don't need teachers who resent showing up each day.

But, if you love your job and the impact you get to make each day, then stay and keep changing lives.

What do you think your students think of you? Go ahead, be honest. You're allowed to say nice things about yourself here.

DAY FIFTY-FIVE

Remember, clear communication is vital to successful outcomes in all areas of life. Our comments, tone, facial expressions, and body language can give hope and light or take hope and light away.

If we look closely enough, we can see how we make someone feel when communicating with them. If we dull the glimmers in their eyes as they look into ours, we probably need to change our communication.

Smile and speak with hope in your voice. You never know whose light you will ignite.

Good vibes are contagious! What specific communication can you use with others to bring out the best in them?

DAY FIFTY-SIX

Bullying doesn't only happen with kids. Bullying occurs in our adult lives, too. Unfortunately, educational settings can be places where adult bullying often occurs.

It is our responsibility to stand up for ourselves and not allow anyone to be bullied by another. It is our job to report bullying behavior by adults. Put it this way: If an adult is bullying another adult, they are more than likely not being kind to kids, either. We are not in high school anymore; we cannot condone behavior that lessens another person's value.

Emotional intelligence allows us to respond to and report injustices around us responsibly, powerfully, and adequately.

How do you respond to adult bullying situations? How can you use your emotional intelligence to be a more responsible advocate for everyone around you?

DAY FIFTY-SEVEN

A culture doesn't create itself. We create our cultures—every single one of us. We can also re-create our cultures to be what we want. Here's the secret: We must take responsibility. Shifting a culture might start with only you and your immediate team. Then, what you create can grow into something more.

If we sit back and wait for others to change cultures for us, it will be a long wait. Cultural change takes everyone's efforts, but what if you can ignite that change with your simple actions? Start with your attitude, reactions, and work ethic, and then your positive vibes will creep into your greater community. Remember, our influence can be positive or negative, and that's a lot of personal power to use wisely.

What do you want for your dream culture? How will you take responsibility for working toward that dream culture?

DAY FIFTY-EIGHT

Celebrating all humans is essential in our profession, not only our youth but also our adults. Sometimes, adults can be judgmental and jealous, but we must rise above and remain stable in emotional intelligence.

Everyone deserves to be treated equally and respectfully. As the saying goes, "If you have nothing nice to say, say nothing at all." This motto will help us all.

What can you do to rise above the shade others cast? How can you stop negative talk amongst peers and improve your environment?

DAY FIFTY-NINE

Make today exactly what you want it to be. How do we do this? The first action step is to be who you want to be as a good human. Show up for yourself first. Take care of your own needs and health. Allow these actions to bring in self-love.

The second action step is to think about the humans around you and remember they are *all* going through something difficult. It's life. Allow that thought to bring empathy and love into your heart.

Now that your heart is open, what you want to *be* in your day will show up naturally. Get ready to accept your best moments with open arms.

What action steps can you tackle to make today the best
day?

Action Step 1:

Action Step 2:

DAY SIXTY

It's important to look inward to ensure you are happy where you are, personally and professionally. We know life can't be perfect, but we can evaluate whether where we take up space is where we want to be. As teachers, we should want to be right where we are because too much is at stake. Is it time to move on if we don't want to be where we are?

Personally and professionally, is it time to stay and do our best for the future—or is it time to move on?

DAY SIXTY-ONE

Just like in baseball, if you are playing shortstop, the batter is up, and you say to yourself, "I hope the ball isn't hit to me," you can guarantee that the ball will be hit straight at you.

So, when we go through our days hoping and praying, we don't get walk-throughs or observations; we should know that someone will indeed walk into our space.

If we change our perspective from fear to "bring it," then we are ready for anything that comes our way.

What fears can you turn into "bring it" so you can attract
the best outcomes?

Day Sixty-Two

Some days, we are just tired. We forget our purpose. There are days when we feel like we can't get enough energy to do anything productive.

But then we start teaching.

We see the students connecting, reacting, and learning. We start to smile, and our body wakes up; we are in the moment, and everything makes sense in those moments. This is why we wake up and keep doing our important jobs day in and day out.

These moments are part of your *why*.

What is your *why* for waking up, walking out the door, and working daily for our youth?

DAY SIXTY-THREE

Being brave does not mean we have to know how to conquer all things. It's hard to conquer life's unknowns until we get there, and education is full of unknowns. Being brave means repeatedly showing up—on good and bad days—and doing our best within the unknowns. Because humans depend on us.

Our future depends on us.

What a great reason to give our all and be brave today.

What are three reasons to show up brave today?

DAY SIXTY-FOUR

Ego. We all have one. But how we manage our egos is the magic of emotional intelligence. Our egos can get us in trouble, prevent our growth and the growth of others, and become a weak link in our environments.

If we self-reflect, we can use our egos for good. Celebrate strong team members. Embrace mistakes and learning moments. Understand that we are better with talented humans around us. It's not a competition. We are here to work together for the greater good. We don't have control over much in life, but we do have control over our ego, and we allow our ego to work for us.

How do you celebrate those around you—their ideas and talents? How do they make you better?

DAY SIXTY-FIVE

Where is the love?

I challenge you today to find love where it exists. Where we can find appropriate love, we can find more goodness, open minds, and collaboration. Keep an eye out for kindness, grace, and smiles. Maybe you're the one showing the world what love looks like.

Who in your current environment exudes love: love for their job, teams, and students?

_____

_____

_____

_____

_____

_____

_____

_____

_____

_____

_____

_____

_____

_____

_____

DAY SIXTY-SIX

Be intentional about finding balance in what you want and need while giving others what they need. Pay attention to and care for what you need to survive and thrive. If there are things that you need to change, be intentional about taking steps to make those changes. Nothing happens on its own without action.

Once you figure out your needs and wants, make an action plan for how to acquire them. Initiate the plan and then execute it with action. You wouldn't believe how much control you have over your life events and plans once you set your intentions.

What are your needs or wants?

What are three initiating action steps to move closer to acquiring your needs or wants?

When will you execute your steps?

DAY SIXTY-SEVEN

Staying in the same groups each day at work can sometimes prevent growth. There is certainly comfort in being close to your coworker groups, and many of us might have a best friend within that group. Although this might work for us, we also may need to diversify our engagement at work to support continuous learning, creative ideas, and growth.

On a greater scale of community, the more people we connect with, the fewer silos, resulting in a more unified culture. This does not mean we have to be close to every person. That's not realistic. It's important to have conversations with those outside of our cliques to prevent cliques and promote growth.

Do you collaborate, talk with, or join other groups outside
your immediate group? If not, do you find this limiting?

Day Sixty-Eight

As mentioned in yesterday's writing, we cannot grow unless change is implemented or sprinkled throughout our lives in some form. The same goes for growing through pain, loss, and heartbreak. We don't want to feel these things, but we will grow in some way after we go through the pain. We may not know the reason behind the pain, but remember that there are answers, truth, and growth on the other side of pain. Try to find gratitude for the struggle life delivers.

Gratitude in pain makes us stronger.

What struggles may you be experiencing right now? Can you see growth in the struggle yet? Can you find gratitude for the experience?

DAY SIXTY-NINE

You can do this! You were meant to care for and love our future, which is before you each day—our youth.

At the same time, you were meant to care for and love yourself. In fact, we can't take care of our future without taking care of ourselves first.

How are you taking care of yourself these days?

DAY SEVENTY

Making our days better can only depend on us. Sure, we can wait around on others to make us feel better, but we might be waiting a long time, and that's precious time passing us by! We should try to make others feel valued, but we can't depend on the same from others. If it happens, great, but we must find value for ourselves first. When this happens, we can soar through life without need. The kudos from those who see and appreciate us will come at the right time.

Do you value yourself or depend on others to give you value? If you rely on others, how can you shift your mindset?

DAY SEVENTY-ONE

This is the time of year when exhaustion is our first thought in the morning as we open our eyes. But we still get up, take one step in front of the other, grab our coffee or energy shake, and walk out the door.

Why? Because our future is waiting for us! That makes you essential. Is there anything more important than serving our future generations?

High five on digging deep and showing up today!

How are you feeling today? Are there any intentional mindset changes you could make in order to feel better?

_____

_____

_____

_____

_____

_____

_____

_____

_____

_____

_____

_____

_____

_____

_____

_____

_____

DAY SEVENTY-TWO

There are days when we are irritated and often don't even know why. The students get on our nerves, the adults anger us, and leadership frustrates us. We go home, and our irritation often bleeds into our personal lives. Whew . . . It's a lot, and how we manage these emotions might be less than desirable.

Remember, we *all* still have hormones kicking around all over the place. But mostly, we are human. We all have these days, and it's our responsibility to find the reasons behind them and figure out how to move past them without drama or ruining relationships.

How can you consciously move out of these times more
efficiently and with less drama?

DAY SEVENTY-THREE

Just as we get irritated and tired during this time of year, so do our students. They are overwhelmed, and finding the motivation to get out of bed is tough. There may be yelling in the morning, or they might have had a rough night. The truth is, we never know what our students are going through.

What we know for certain is that how we communicate as adults can have a lasting impact on them and maybe turn their days or lives around. If we, as adults, have a terrible day, we have developed tools to control our behavior. Our youth's tools are evolving. They need us to be an example of making others feel better, not pushing our issues on them.

Can you be a stable human for our youth by being a consistent force? How can you lead by example?

(By the way, other adults are watching, too.)

DAY SEVENTY-FOUR

Take a moment and look into the eyes of the students you serve. If you do, you will remember your *why*: Why do you stay in an education system that often feels like it fails us all? Why do you make ends meet financially? Why your heart has been able to grow hundreds of times over. One single person can remind us each day of our *why* . . . if we pay attention.

Look for your *why* today. What was it?

DAY SEVENTY-FIVE

Take a gratitude walk today. I know you think you don't have time, but I dare you to make the time—step outside of your regular routine. Create a new habit. Go solo or grab a friend, but take a walk. In these walks, we can forget about the papers to grade, that meeting we dread, or the room to clean. Feel your body move. Get out of your brain space and into your heart space. Gratitude walks remind us of life holistically.

Remember, gratitude has the power to uplift and bring hope. No other emotion can coexist with gratitude. It is the light in the dark times.

What time will you intentionally take a short walk today?
How will you hold yourself accountable?

_____

_____

_____

_____

_____

_____

_____

_____

_____

_____

_____

_____

_____

_____

DAY SEVENTY-SIX

Yesterday, we chatted about taking a short gratitude walk daily to clear your brain and energy. No matter your work ethic or how much you tell yourself, "I just don't have time," . . . it is plausible to make time.

Those of us who say, "I don't have time for anything," are choosing not to have time for anything. This is the balancing act that we are responsible for in our lives.

The brave thing to do is not to hide behind your work but rather figure out strategies to take healthy breaks and shift your focus for a moment. We are not given kudos for how hard we work when it might negatively affect our work. Balance is key to a strong and successful work ethic.

Do you find yourself saying, "I don't have time"? Is this true? Really?

DAY SEVENTY-SEVEN

Some days are full of joy, and others are simply painful, depending on the day's events. From the moment we wake up in the morning until we close our eyes at night, a hundred different events have taken place. In one minute of time, our feelings can change from happy to angry— depending on circumstances. We are human, and we are in the service industry. Although admirable work, it doesn't mean we should lose ourselves in service. Within our career, we can get lost in the "it's for the kids" mindset. We work so hard that we exhaust ourselves and deplete our energy.

Save some of your energy for other things in life. Try not to lose yourself in your work. It's not worth it. Service to others does not mean we give everything we have away. Take care of yourself and your own life first. Diversify your life experiences. Live.

Have you lost yourself in your job? Is it worth it?

DAY SEVENTY-EIGHT

There's a fine line between giving our all and giving away everything we have.

As teachers, we can lose ourselves in our work before realizing it. The responsibility is so great that we devote everything, sometimes even more.

This is where burnout comes into play. We might find ourselves becoming numb so that we can move through the days. Our students notice, and our home life feels it. You have other skills and talents outside of work; use them.

What are your gifts and talents outside of work?

DAY SEVENTY-NINE

What have you done for yourself lately? Yes, money might be tight. Maybe you are exhausted each night and on the weekends. But it's important to balance work and your home life, even if you start with small things.

Try leaving your laptop at work. Take a short walk around your neighborhood block, walk around a community art market, or take yourself out for your favorite beverage or meal. When we don't get outside of our work environment, we will find ourselves limited in happiness. We might even enter a state of depression.

Dig deep and love yourself by experiencing life outside of work so happiness can remain consistent.

What have you done for yourself lately that has nothing to
do with work?

DAY EIGHTY

Today, you get to see people around you differently. You get to let go of judgments. You get to forgive. You get to release grudges. Everyone around you is human. They have stories, losses, trauma, love, and struggles. Each day, we all have an opportunity to let go of our pain, insecurities, and judgments and treat others respectfully to live this life the best they can. In return, we will receive the same treatment. We give not only because we want to receive but because it's the right thing to do for humans. These days, our environments need each of us to show up with grace and understanding.

How can you show up with more grace and understanding today?

DAY EIGHTY-ONE

It's true. Adults can be as petty as the mean girl cliques and bullies from our early school days. Why does this still happen? Some humans do not develop emotionally past high school. You can do nothing to change that about others, but we can change how we react as adults.

We can choose not to let these individuals get in our heads. We can choose to change who we are and how we act toward others. We don't allow them to dictate how we show up each day. It's not worth it. Life is too short to be stuck in someone else's developmental stagnation.

If we are the ones still acting like we are in high school— talking behind people's backs and hurting others—the mirror is waiting for us to ask ourselves tough questions.

Is it worth worrying about those who still judge others in adulthood? How can you prevent this behavior from negatively impacting your life?

DAY EIGHTY-TWO

Be the leader you dream others would be for you. Although you may not be interested in having the job of the highest-ranking leader at your school or district, you still have every right to be an amazing leader. The truth is that many of us do not have access to our hierarchical leaders because they are too busy. The humans we have the most access to are on our immediate teams, and we can be leaders among those individuals. It takes us all acting as leaders to keep things moving in the right direction.

Don't be afraid to be a leader among leaders.

In what ways do you demonstrate leadership in your
position?

DAY EIGHTY-THREE

How are you communicating with others? How are you entering conversations? How are you leaving conversations? Are we leaving others feeling heavy or lifted? Are we attentive to our tone, facial expressions, and body language? The vibe we exude can be a game changer in making or breaking another person's day. No matter the age of the people we enter into conversation with, we must ensure that we are responsible for leaving good vibes.

We never know when we have given hope to someone who has lost hope internally.

How are you keeping your communication positive?

DAY EIGHTY-FOUR

Every day that we arrive at work, we have an opportunity to bring light to others. We can also bring darkness to others. We get to choose which one. No one else is responsible for our energy. It's all on us. If we show our light, even when we don't feel like it, we not only help those around us, but we also change our own lives each day.

Can you let go of negativity long enough to be the light for others around you?

DAY EIGHTY-FIVE

Do you know those students who look up to you? The ones who are watching your every move?

Let them see your best today. Smile when you don't feel like it. Praise them when you want to scream. Walk alongside them instead of in front of them. Let them feel that they matter and that they are the reason you keep showing up. Our influence is open-ended.

In what ways do you personally impact those around you on a daily basis?

DAY EIGHTY-SIX

When a student smiles at you, it's because they trust you. They might need a smile in return, or maybe they know you need a smile. Perhaps they see you stressed or feel your pain. Be intentional today about *seeing* those humans around you who *see* you. They love you. Let them know you appreciate their efforts, even if that appreciation is shown as a smile in return.

Is there someone you might be hard on who needs you to really see them today?

DAY EIGHTY-SEVEN

The service work of being a teacher is "human work" and can sometimes challenge our moral compass. We give so much daily, yet the return feels like a fraction of what we give away. This can skew our outlook. Working in this industry somehow trains our brains to think we should be doing all this good work without any thanks in return. But we are human and need to be seen, heard, and thanked, which leads to feeling valued.

Thank you for what you do every day.

Do you feel you receive enough gratitude from those around you, your leaders, and yourself?

DAY EIGHTY-EIGHT

Depending on what happens in our personal lives, we may show up to work with a different outlook, attitude, tolerance, and behavior.

Something that may not be a big deal one day may send us over the edge on another day because of what we are feeling internally. The same goes for the humans around us. Finding grace for ourselves and those around us is the nicest thing we can do for everyone and our cultures.

How can you stop and remind yourself to find grace for
yourself and others on tough days?

_____

_____

_____

_____

_____

_____

_____

_____

_____

_____

_____

_____

_____

_____

_____

DAY EIGHTY-NINE

Our influence is powerful and endless. We get to be core memories for so many humans who are growing around us. If you are the teacher everyone remembers when they are in adulthood, how will they remember you? What is your legacy? We always have eyes watching us, and we owe it to those watching to be our most loving, supportive, and safest selves. We have to be our best for them to find their best.

What legacy do you want to leave for those who will remember you?

DAY NINETY

You made it! Half way! Getting to this point in your school year is difficult, so let's talk about preservation. It is our responsibility to preserve ourselves while working in the educational field. It can genuinely suck us dry of all we have. It can leave us with nothing left to give ourselves and our family. Preservation means to protect yourself and save energy for yourself. Saying no is one of the best routes to self-preservation. Say no to things that aren't feeding your soul. Say no to taking work home. Say no to staying late.

Say yes to yourself.

How will you say yes to yourself today and for the rest of this school year?

_____

_____

_____

_____

_____

_____

_____

_____

_____

_____

_____

_____

_____

_____

_____

_____

_____

DAY NINETY-ONE

Mindful communication and actions will not only make someone else's day but can also make your day. It does not matter how someone else decides to go about life; it's about how we go about our own lives. How are we approaching life so we can be proud of each day when we lay our heads down at night?

The beauty of mindfulness is that when we show up mindful each day, others can trust us more. They know what to expect from us. There are no surprises. This, in turn, makes others around us feel safe. Feeling safe is the foundation for amazing growth.

How are you showing up mindful of others in your life and for yourself?

_____

_____

_____

_____

_____

_____

_____

_____

_____

_____

_____

_____

_____

_____

_____

_____

_____

DAY NINETY-TWO

There are days when our emotional intelligence doesn't show its highest capabilities. This could be due to hormones, life changes, stress, anxiety, or fear. Emotional intelligence (EQ) is not something that we automatically have within us. It's a work in progress.

Part of EQ is knowing when others do not have it and being aware enough not to get sucked into their lack of emotional intelligence at work. You know how we tell the kids not to be followers and run into a burning house because someone else does? We need to listen to our own advice.

We can grow in our EQ by having control of how we react to others and situations. Rising above the petty words, actions, and vibes of human interaction and being intentional about how our words, actions, and vibes affect others is a big part of obtaining consistent emotional intelligence.

Have you ever wondered about your emotional intelligence?
Are you caught up in the drama, or are you the calm,
rational voice amid chaos?

DAY NINETY-THREE

Failure is inevitable. Being told no is part of life. It is hard for us as adults to manage being told no. We strive to understand our own and others' actions through social intelligence. Social intelligence is not how social or anti-social we are. Social intelligence is learned, and just like emotional intelligence, we aren't automatically born with this type of intellect.

EQ and social intelligence involve how we react, resolve, and recount life events. Failure and success are where our social intelligence grows and matures. If we can better understand the actions of those around us and our own, we can learn how to cope, coexist, and remain focused—be better socially. We can't control what anyone does but can control how we respond by recognizing successes and failures as learning opportunities.

How do you rate your social intelligence at work? How are you learning from your failures and successes?

DAY NINETY-FOUR

Resilience is part of our journey in education. Resilience is not endurance, as we might think. Having endurance means we continuously need to get through challenges and experiences.

Resilience means we have figured out how to bounce back from difficult situations and challenges quickly and then move on. In education, we often don't know what's coming our way minute to minute. While endurance is essential, it can exhaust us and send us into burnout mode. Practicing resilience can be one of our most efficient tools to keep us healthier throughout our days and school year.

Where are you in the resilience vs endurance challenge?
How can you shift your mindset to have more long-term
energy with the tool of resilience?

DAY NINETY-FIVE

You have the power to shape young minds and create a lasting impact, but power can be a tricky tool. Power is a human need that is directly connected to control. We all have this need in some form: the need to control ourselves or the environment around us. This power can be your superpower or your demise.

We must be careful, mindful, and safe with each power level. In education, we should use our power to better our communities and inspire those who look up to us. We cannot use this power to harm; this is the worst use of power.

This profession does not need humans who use their power to cause problems and stress for others. We are responsible for being role models of balanced power so those around us can extend the energy into the world and improve our future. That's how far our superpower extends!

How do you use your power? What is your superpower in education?

DAY NINETY-SIX

Your passion for teaching and leading is contagious. Young and old, others can pick up on your energy a mile away and generally trust those whose passion is pure and consistent.

While on the rollercoaster of education, creating consistency in our flow is the golden standard. With consistency, those around us know what to expect. There's no question of how you might contribute on any given day.

One way to obtain consistency in life is to be more proactive and less reactive to life events.

Are you typically proactive or reactive to life events? Do others consider you a consistent presence each day?

_____

_____

_____

_____

_____

_____

_____

_____

_____

_____

_____

_____

_____

_____

_____

_____

_____

DAY NINETY-SEVEN

We can inspire others daily with our words as we enter our classrooms, hallways, offices, or playgrounds. No matter the age of the humans around us, we can use our influence and encouraging words to motivate. Imagine if we made it a daily habit to compliment, notice, and share uplifting words with those around us.

This type of practice alone could shift a culture for the better. Each of us can shift the culture in which we live and work. We can use our power to be negative and bring the cultural energy down, or we can be the light.

There can never be too much positivity in the world.

Are you a light for others? Are you sharing encouraging words to motivate humans around you?

DAY NINETY-EIGHT

Be the person who invites others to sit with you. Whether in group meetings or lunch, try to help others feel welcome. Any environment where humans interact allows them to feel like they belong or are daily visitors.

For more introverted individuals, the education profession can be daunting. Although introverted individuals can be some of the best teachers for our youth within the classroom, sometimes adulting is hard.

Being inclusive and welcoming to all humans around us is how our culture expands to its greatest capacity. Collective cultures are not made up of cliques that exclude.

What can you do today to include someone new? If you are an introvert yourself, what can you do to enter your school society a little more?

DAY NINETY-NINE

Be the social group that does not talk behind someone's back when they leave the table or room. We are better than this.

Along these lines, it's better to sit alone than join a group of people you know will talk about you when you leave. How do you know they will? Because they do it to everyone else.

Save yourself some drama and join a group where you feel accepted and appreciated and the vibe is authentic. We work with amazing humans, and we stick with those individuals who are genuine and honest.

How do you see yourself navigating social group situations at work?

Day One Hundred

Thank you for making it to this point in the school year. In one hundred days, you have shown up, filled minds, helped others, saved lives, and given back to our society with your gifts.

You've made it to the top of the rollercoaster, and it should feel downwind and fast from here on out. Take a deep breath, pat yourself on the heart, order out for lunch or dinner, and thank yourself for what you do each day.

What will your focus be for the rest of the year? What will your legacy be after this year?

DAY ONE HUNDRED ONE

Something that helps our teams thrive is acknowledging the skills and abilities of others around you. Give them kudos! In our profession, there is no time for jealousy or envy. We all work hard, get paid poorly, and should see each other as equals no matter the status of our job titles.

We should always be providing space for teammates to develop their skills. This not only makes each individual stronger, but it makes our teams healthier. With this type of teamwork, those we serve will benefit from our team dynamics.

Who's on your immediate team? What are their skills and talents? How can you acknowledge their skills and talents?

DAY ONE HUNDRED TWO

At this point in the year, you've had enough time to reflect on if you have kept your promises and managed your expectations of yourself and others. Two of the most important ways to gain the trust of others around us are to do what we say we are going to do and to keep our expectations balanced.

Our capacity can only stretch so far, and when we stretch our capacity to its limits, our follow-through may be poor. When we don't follow through on even the most minor promises, those around us, old and young, lose their trust. When we say, "I will" or "we will," we need to make these things happen. Otherwise, try not to say these things out loud and keep things private until you are 100% sure you can follow through.

How are you doing this year in following through on your promises to yourself and others? What are your realistic expectations for fulfilling promises made?

DAY ONE HUNDRED THREE

Sometimes, our teams around us don't know anything about us, and you don't know about them. Educational intelligence is not only centered around academics. This reminds us that cultural intelligence can become a skill that takes us further into our success. Cultural intelligence (CQ) is something to dig further into, but some examples of CQ are:

- Developing an awareness of our differences and our biases toward those differences.
- Self-awareness is essential, especially in how we relate to others within our diverse cultures.
- Be eager to learn more about the people around us and celebrate varied cultures and traditions.
- Keep an open mind and let go of judgments.
- Put ourselves in different groups to try to understand others around us.

There is much more to acquiring cultural intelligence, but this can get the ball rolling.

Where are you in cultural intelligence on a scale of 1–5, with 5 being the strongest level? What can you do to dig deeper into this type of intelligence?

DAY ONE HUNDRED FOUR

When groups of humans gather, there's bound to be some toxic behavior from someone around us—it might even be us. This is a reminder that it is our choice to mingle with toxicity or not. We, as adults, have a voice and the power to walk away from toxic behavior.

Typically, when toxic behavior starts affecting others, it is not personal to anyone else. It is a reflection of what that human is going through internally. We can give grace and empathy, but at the same time, we can remove ourselves from that energy. This is another way to remain in a positive headspace for those we serve.

Do you have anyone you must give grace to and distance yourself from? Is there any relationship you need to reevaluate?

DAY ONE HUNDRED FIVE

The amazing thing about communities is that we get to do life together—the ups and downs and in-betweens. We celebrate together and grieve together. Within education, we have unique communities where we can participate and support each other's lives.

Today, let's celebrate our community in all its good ways and be grateful for the workspace that gives us a reason to come to work each day. Tell someone *thank you* today for being part of your tribe for at least 180 days of the year.

How are you grateful for your work community? Who do you want to thank today and why?

DAY ONE HUNDRED SIX

Today, while we are changing the world and coming up with creative ideas and plans, remember to leave space for others to be creative and have important ideas. A sign of a good leader—and we are one—is to let others around us have great ideas and plans and let them know we support them while also letting them teach us sometimes. The skill of listening comes in handy today.

This is how we grow as a team in the most productive ways.

How will you take time to sit back and listen today?

DAY ONE HUNDRED SEVEN

We all have weak moments, make mistakes, and are given opportunities to learn from them. Are we giving others enough space to make mistakes and not have to pay for them long-term? Are we giving ourselves and others around us second chances? We are all learning each and every day. We are figuring out how to navigate situations and events as we move along in life. Today, someone will have a weak moment, and we will be there to coach them along the way in the most positive way. These moments change lives.

What is your commitment today to honoring human mistakes and giving grace where needed?

DAY ONE HUNDRED EIGHT

Let me remind you of *why* you came to work today. Someone needs you, your smile, and the knowledge that you *see* them. We don't know if this person is someone we work with or a student we serve, but it will be someone.

This afternoon, someone will go home and talk about you. They will share how much you made their day and that they believe in themselves a little more. Their heart will be happier because you chose to show up and be your best.

How will you be more present and mindful today?

_____

_____

_____

_____

_____

_____

_____

_____

_____

_____

_____

_____

_____

_____

_____

_____

DAY ONE HUNDRED NINE

Writing letters of gratitude is a meaningful way to let someone know that you care and appreciate them. We often get little thanks at work, but when someone shares their appreciation, it can make our day, week, or year.

Sure, you can send an email. That works, but what if you took the time to write out the gratitude notes and hand-delivered them?

The challenge is to write one gratitude note for someone this week and try to make it a habit for each week or month. Tell them why you are grateful for them. One sentence is all you need.

To whom will you write your gratitude note this week and why?

DAY ONE HUNDRED TEN

Something good is going to happen around you today. Keep your eyes open for amazing things to come your way because you have been practicing everything in this book, and you are a good human.

All of that energy that you give each day comes back around. So, we should probably invest in good energy. Look around at the changes you make and the smiles you bring to others.

Have you been investing in good energy lately, or not so good? If your energy has been wonky lately, how can you shift it?

DAY ONE HUNDRED ELEVEN

Tired? Yep, it's a reality for everyone at this point in the year.

One way to keep our spirits high and our perspectives open-minded is to keep learning. Sometimes, when we don't know what's wrong with us but are in a rut, learning something new can free up our energy. This does not have to be returning to school and getting another degree. Reading articles daily or taking a professional development course that genuinely matters to you can bring back your spark. Even if you don't feel in a rut, filling your mind with new information can help you become a wiser educator.

Most of us are educators because we know how necessary knowledge is for all humans. So, find something that interests you and keep learning. If we aren't learning, we're dying. To learn is to grow.

What are simple ways you can keep growing by gaining new knowledge?

DAY ONE HUNDRED TWELVE

Education is a beast! This is why we take breaks in the summer. It is 180 days of focus, nose to the grindstone, managing, teaching, listening, giving, and loving. We exude so much emotion in a 180-day race to the end.

At this time, we might find ourselves out of balance because we are not adequately caring for ourselves. Remember to keep life as balanced as possible. Although teaching is the most important job in the world, it can't be our everything. Each day, be intentional about ways to do things for yourself—not your job or those you serve. There has to be separation within all we do so that every part of our lives has the opportunity to serve us and others.

What small shifts can you make in your life right now to serve yourself while giving so much to others?

DAY ONE HUNDRED THIRTEEN

Water is the source of life that we all need. As educators, let's face it: there is little time to even go to the bathroom, let alone drink water for our health. We often go home and feel almost dehydrated because of how much we have talked, managed, and walked. During our days, we might not be taking time to nourish our bodies with water.

Drinking more water is a simple action that can change brain cell activity, muscle engagement, and energy levels. It is part of our balancing act that we should insist on accomplishing each day to actively help ourselves feel better.

What is your plan of action around drinking more water? What motivates you to follow through with this action plan?

DAY ONE HUNDRED FOURTEEN

What's your mindset today? When you woke up this morning, I hope you realized you would make someone's day today by going to work. Someone is looking forward to seeing only you out of everyone else today. You are probably the reason someone got out of bed and took steps forward. You are cherished by many and those around you are lucky to have you in their lives—if only for a brief moment in time.

You are important.

How did you wake up this morning? How do you feel now?
It's a choice.

DAY ONE HUNDRED FIFTEEN

Did you know that the talents within us naturally exist and are predispositions? Our talents can be at all levels, but our skills are different. Skill is acquired. When we teach or lead in any capacity, we are responsible for acquiring more knowledge, practicing new skills, and letting our natural talents brew underneath it all. Our strength as humans and professionals comes from sharing our natural talent, acquired skills, and knowledge.

How will you keep becoming stronger as a human and professional with your natural talents, acquired skills, and knowledge?

DAY ONE HUNDRED SIXTEEN

You have a story about how you got to where you are today. It's probably no accident that you are where you are in this moment in life, and it's also no accident that you are in the lives of those around you. Maybe being in education isn't what you dreamed for your life, or you feel your purpose is more than this. Perhaps you had bigger dreams, and things got in the way. Life happened.

Is there a bigger purpose in life than educating our future? There's no better way to know for sure that you have changed the world in some way than to be an educator.

What were your dreams for yourself? How would those dreams have changed the world? Does it compare to your span of influence now?

Day One Hundred Seventeen

You are still here, working within education with its ups and downs. How interesting. There must be some reason you keep showing up each day. Your heart is enormous, and you are a giver. It's not the fault of those we serve that our educational system is less than stellar. They are simply trying to get an education and do what they need to do to progress in life. Even in a profession that doesn't have many perks, you are devoted to the original mission: to make our world better through education.

Thank you.

Why are you still here?

DAY ONE HUNDRED EIGHTEEN

Joy is so underrated. Joy can show up in a brief second or for minutes at a time. Sometimes, we let time pass by without recognizing the rare beauty of these joy-filled moments.

Today, there might be a lot of joyful moments to notice. Whatever you do, stop, breathe in these joyful moments, give a word of gratitude, and know that you deserve it. You are deserving of all good things, so this is a reminder to accept these gifts life gives you and the moments you help create.

What are all of the fantastic reasons you deserve joy-filled moments?

DAY ONE HUNDRED NINETEEN

Some days are a drag—they just are. We can use positive psychology as hard as possible, but some days are just bad. With the good, there will be bad; with giving, there will be pain. The only thing that can give us hope is that tomorrow will be a new day, and we will always grow with pain. Still, it's important to recognize bad days and why they are bad. It's okay to sit in the moment of a rough day, but don't linger too long. There's work to be done, and we always have control of our mindsets. Always.

Have you had a bad day lately? Why was it bad? Did you shift your mindset to cope?

DAY ONE HUNDRED TWENTY

Beyond the hustle and bustle of a day, outside of grading papers or managing schools, there is peace in knowing that we make a difference each day that we decide to give our all. We should feel calm when we close our eyes at night, knowing we have done our best. Tomorrow will bring new challenges, but today, we did our best.

Tomorrow is full of unknowns, so losing sleep tonight over what might happen tomorrow doesn't benefit us. Getting some rest will make it possible to be sharp, aware, and not so cranky.

What will you tell yourself when your mind is racing and you can't get to sleep because of work?

DAY ONE HUNDRED TWENTY-ONE

Take a moment this morning to think about those you serve. Choose a single person. Imagine them moving through grade levels, becoming stronger and wiser. See them making choices for themselves and helping others. Watch them walk across the stage for graduation, go out into the world, and make a difference in our communities.

You planted a seed for that person to grow. Take credit for that, and know that each human you serve will take something you gave with them. How remarkable!

Were you able to envision these scenarios? Were you able to feel your contribution to their story?

Day One Hundred Twenty-Two

Knowing our capacity to manage things is an important part of being successful. It doesn't feel good when we overcommit and can't give what we've promised. We also cheat ourselves and others out of something someone else could do better. Remember, saying no is brave and healthy when we can't give our best, and someone else might do the job we committed to better, and that's perfectly okay. Share the work.

Sometimes, it takes failing to understand our capacity better. Maintaining a healthy balance is knowing ourselves and what we can handle. When we stay within the limits of our capacity, we win, and others win. Showing adult maturity in knowing and managing our limitations makes us function at a higher level.

Do you generally know your capacity limits? Do you stay within them? Or do you go over the limits?

DAY ONE HUNDRED TWENTY-THREE

Studies have shown that when we practice gratitude, our well-being improves, and our mindset is more positive. While leading others, it is important to be role models in the ways we wish to see others. Practicing gratitude can settle harsh feelings and help others feel like they belong and are accepted. A simple *thank you* can make our environments less on edge, more inclusive, and a space where those around us feel seen and valued.

It's important to remember that even when things don't go as planned, there are always valuable lessons, unseen blessings, and growth opportunities to be found. These adverse events are not setbacks, but stepping stones to a brighter future.

Who needs to be seen with kudos or a thank you in your work life?

_____

_____

_____

_____

_____

_____

_____

_____

_____

_____

_____

_____

_____

Day One Hundred Twenty-Four

The human brain is incredible. Each human is firing off eighty-six billion neurons at any given moment to help process information and create thoughts. Think about that with those around you. Look how much energy is being exuded into our work and living space. Although we are designed for this neuron action to occur, this can be exhaustive for some, depending on how we process information. That's what makes each of us unique and perfect.

Sometimes, we can get frustrated with how fast or slow someone is processing or learning. Celebrating each brain is where we can make others and ourselves feel seen, heard, and loved. Celebrating neurodiversity is our job. There is no right way to think, behave, or learn.

Today, how can you celebrate every human around you by meeting them where their neurons fire and how they process and learn?

_____

_____

_____

_____

_____

_____

_____

_____

_____

_____

_____

_____

_____

_____

_____

DAY ONE HUNDRED TWENTY-FIVE

Some have said that teachers have an easy job with an 8 a.m.–4 p.m. workday and summers off. As the saying goes, "Until you've walked a mile in someone's shoes,". . . don't make assumptions.

Teaching is more than a profession. It is a lifestyle in which we never stop thinking about those we serve, how to do things better, and what to do next. At the same time that we are teaching, we are managing behavior, taking care of those who are sick, building character, and being a constant influence in their lives. It is a full-time expenditure of our time, resources, and emotions. The summer is necessary for restoring, learning, and caring for our personal lives. Our profession is not for the faint of heart or weak-minded.

You are a superhero.

Summer is coming soon.

It's never too soon to start planning for summer. What summer plans can you make right now to motivate yourself to get through the next stretch of this school year? Dream away, superhero!

DAY ONE HUNDRED TWENTY-SIX

Say this confidently,

"I am exactly where I need to be today."

We often don't know why things happen, why we meet someone, or why we land where we land in life. Chances are, there is a big story behind where you are today. We may not see the connected dots until we intentionally sit and think through the journey.

With all of the unknowns, the one thing we can count on is love. Love probably landed you where you are today in some form or fashion. On the days you question why, know that you belong right where you are for now.

What are the connected dots in your story that got you to today?

_____

_____

_____

_____

_____

_____

_____

_____

_____

_____

_____

_____

_____

_____

_____

_____

_____

DAY ONE HUNDRED TWENTY-SEVEN

Today feels like a good day to let it all out. Things are upsetting you, and some things need to change around you. This will always be the case when so many humans work together. So, today, you can let out your frustrations right here; if you let them out here, maybe others won't pick up on your lack of jubilance out there.

Feeling this way is natural. Let it out, do what you can to create the change you think is needed, and let it go. There are some things we have no control over.

What do you need to let out? Write in code, draw pictures, and do what you must, but let it out so you can move forward.

DAY ONE HUNDRED TWENTY-EIGHT

Life can surely throw some good curve balls when we least expect it. As educators, when life throws us a hardship, we still have to show up to work and act like nothing is wrong. So many people of all ages depend on us. We should show up with a smile, strength, and guidance. They don't have time for us to be sad, cry, or unfocused.

In our profession, we must keep our eye on the ball and keep it positive for 180 days. This is exhausting, but you do it well. Please make sure this afternoon, when no one is depending on you for longer than five minutes, that you take a deep breath and remind yourself that you are human.

A super-human!

What are life's curve balls right now?

Day One Hundred Twenty-Nine

Many educators care for and make daily decisions for others, then go home to care for their families. There's never a break. You not only go to work for those you serve, but you also go to work to support your family. Kudos to you for making it all work. Thank you for being an extraordinary caregiver.

No one does it all quite like you!

How do you do it all? What keeps you going when you're caring for so many people every day?

DAY ONE HUNDRED THIRTY

There's someone at work with whom you need to make amends sooner rather than later. There's no need to befriend the person, but clearing the air is a healthy choice. There are many people in our lives we do not need, and that's perfectly okay. Keeping our boundaries is one of the most important things we can do in our work engagements. Keeping things professional is best practice at work, and those few people you let in will either work out or they won't.

It's admirable and brave to go to the person you have issues with and settle them. Be the emotionally intelligent party who needs to move on from drama. Life is too short, and your energy is too good for drama to taint your life.

We don't want things like this to hold us back from living our lives to the fullest.

(If this doesn't pertain to you and you know someone it does pertain to, please share).

What's the issue? How long has this been going on? What can you do to solve the problem while keeping your boundaries?

DAY ONE HUNDRED THIRTY-ONE

Time is rare these days. Have you noticed how fast it's flying by? In another month or so, you will reflect on this year and think, "That went so fast." But the truth is, we have some very long days as educators. A dozen unusual things can happen to us in one day, and some events are on the level of triage.

You are good at managing all sorts of life events throughout the day. Thank you for making everyone around you feel safe. Make sure you stop and take a breather along the way. Enjoy your weekends and take your time with what matters most to you. As important as our jobs are, education can swallow us whole if we let it. Remember to balance home and work so you don't look back and wish you had balanced things better.

How can you balance your home- and work life better?

Day One Hundred Thirty-Two

Believing in yourself is not just a personal trait; it's a professional necessity. Just as we instill confidence in those we educate, we must cultivate our self-belief. You have the power to achieve anything you set your mind to, just like your students.

We forget this as we mature and move into our profession. We might get stuck in patterns and routines, and although structure is a good thing, we forget to look outside our lifestyle routines.

Don't forget about any dreams you might have living inside of you. As a dedicated educator, while you nurture lives daily, you can also contribute magnificently to your personal life and nurture those dreams.

What dreams and talents lie within you, waiting to be nurtured?

DAY ONE HUNDRED THIRTY-THREE

We all have talents and gifts. But what do we do with them? How do we use them? Do we keep them to ourselves? Give them to others? Share with others? Let's be clear: *Sharing* our gifts is very different from *giving* them.

When we share our gifts, we get to keep them as our own, which naturally helps guard against over-giving. We can often give so much in our profession that we are left with little to nothing. But sharing allows us to give what we want and keep what we want and need for ourselves—deciding if we will *give* or *share* our gifts could be a game-changer for our lives and balance.

How do you use your gifts? Do you *give* or *share* them?

DAY ONE HUNDRED THIRTY-FOUR

We are tired and have worked hard, but we can see the light at the end of this year's tunnel. When we feel more exhausted than usual, it's always a good reminder to keep our boundaries strong. Holding appropriate boundaries can be a lot of work. Sometimes, it seems easier to say yes and move on. But can we actually serve the *yes*?

Staying firm in our values and having integrity is more important than ever. Staying strong in our focus is what keeps professionalism at the forefront. We can't be less now; we must dig deep with integrity to finish strong.

In what ways can you hold your boundaries stronger and uphold your commitments to the fullest?

DAY ONE HUNDRED THIRTY-FIVE

We all have dreams outside of our day-to-day lives. Even if we love our careers, most of us want to experience diversity in our occupations. Sometimes, this means we return to school or leave our profession to find something else that makes us happy. But many of us stay in education because it gives us what we need while exploring other paths on our time off.

The point is that if there is something else we feel we need to fill our bucket, we have the power to pursue it.

Where are you now, and where do you want to go? How will you get there?

DAY ONE HUNDRED THIRTY-SIX

Are you not feeling understood by others? There's a remedy
for that.

Try understanding others first. We must understand the
people and things around us before we can be understood. If
we constantly complain about someone else's decisions or
try to outsmart the system, we will never be understood
because we have not done our part for our culture.

Granted, there will be times when we disagree and need to
advocate for ourselves. But if we take time to understand the
policies, missions, and people around us first, we'll soon be
heard and understood.

Where can you work on better understanding a policy, mission, or person in your workplace?

DAY ONE HUNDRED THIRTY-SEVEN

Sharing our emotions appropriately can allow amazing things to enter our lives. However, we cannot share our emotions safely unless we have created space for others to share their emotions safely.

Being a safe place where others know they can share is rare and sacred. Although we must have boundaries, these spaces allow others to feel like they belong and all of us can learn better in these spaces.

Fill in the blank:

I feel _____ today.

I know _____ today.

I love _____ today.

I should _____ today.

I need _____ today.

I don't like _____ today.

I want to change _____ today.

I am grateful for _____ today.

I am inspired by _____ today.

I showed up for _____ today.

DAY ONE HUNDRED THIRTY-EIGHT

If you've been having a hard few days, remember that getting out of your headspace and into your physical being can help you have better energy and moods. Try taking a walk in the middle of the day. It can be a gratitude walk or a walk to feel your body moving. Try listening to music during lunch or learning something from YouTube.

You are in control of choosing more tough days or helping yourself move out of this space by moving your body and brain in a different direction.

What will you decide to do today to shift your energy, and how will you promise to follow through?

DAY ONE HUNDRED THIRTY-NINE

It's a good day to thank others for something—anything. Research shows that writing letters can create connections and help us clarify what we want to say, understand others better, show value, and be inspired.

If you think about how much you appreciate someone, email or write them a note explaining why you appreciate them. When we authentically show gratitude, the other person can receive it, and you will probably change their day for the better. We know how much we love it when others appreciate us, so let's do it first and create healthy connections.

Who are two humans you want to write a note to today?

Day One Hundred Forty

Don't give up yet. Don't you want to see what will happen if you don't give up? There are humans all around you who need you until the last day of this school year. There's still much to learn, much to smile about, and enough time to shape someone's future.

In education, we have little control and don't always know what to expect from others. But we do know that we have control over our attitudes and behaviors. As adults, our actions significantly matter.

Who inspires you to stay locked in for the next forty days?

DAY ONE HUNDRED FORTY-ONE

You probably already think about things you want to change for the next school year. This is the time to advocate for shifts, changes, or anything you feel will help support you and your teams to be the most productive next year. Self-advocacy does not always come easily, but it's important. No one knows what we want or need unless we share and ask. If you don't advocate for what would make your work life better, then no one will.

The key to successful self-advocacy is to be confident, calm, and patient in the process. Respecting policies and the people around us while we advocate is how we can truly change things. Working *with* the persons who have to make decisions is key. This is not a war or fight; we should communicate like we teach our kids to communicate. Getting feisty doesn't do the trick because decision-makers will shut down and not feel motivated to make changes *with* you.

What needs to change for your next school year to be a success? How will you advocate for yourself in what you need?

DAY ONE HUNDRED FORTY-TWO

No matter the plans that you have for your life, you are meant to be right where you are today. The life lessons and decisions along the way have steered you to the places you stand right now. It is not an accident that you are leading others with your heart and mind. To watch others grow and expand their knowledge because of you is a big responsibility, and you have taken this responsibility seriously.

It's rare to feel like we are where we're supposed to be in life. You are where you belong at this moment, so you might as well soak it up and embrace the moments.

Take a deep breath in and exhale fully. What comes to mind when you fill your lungs?

DAY ONE HUNDRED FORTY-THREE

Sometimes, this space at the end of the year feels like we are in the twilight zone. But, in reality, we are entering the in-between zone. We are ready for summer break, but we are not ready to say goodbye. We are ready for some freedom, but now we feel anxious about the lack of structure. We are excited about vacations, but that puts a hit on finances. We are happy to have space but take summer jobs to make ends meet. We love to binge on series or TV shows, but we need a purpose in life because that's how we operate. If you are a carefree summer educator, kudos to you!

We are all in this in-between zone together.

What are your typical anxieties about having time off in the summer?

_____

_____

_____

_____

_____

_____

_____

_____

_____

_____

_____

_____

_____

_____

_____

DAY ONE HUNDRED FORTY-FOUR

There's a saying, "Leave things better than how we found them." This is a challenge for educators each school year. We are responsible for making big things happen each year in the lives of those we serve. There's another part to this statement that is often missed, "Leave humans we interact with better than how we first met them."

Isn't this what we want for ourselves, our family, and all humans? Imagine if we all left every human better than how they were when we met them. The world would be a better place. This philosophy is a collective effort to do good in the world and a simple way to change how we coexist. Every single thing we do and say matters.

How will you leave things and people around you better than how you found them this year?

DAY ONE HUNDRED FORTY-FIVE

"Practicing failure" sounds like nails on a chalkboard to many of us. Why would anyone in their right mind want to practice failing? Doesn't it come naturally and painfully enough already? Yes, it does feel like we fail enough. Yes, it does feel like we fail much more than we succeed. Your feeling is not wrong. Validating failure in this crazy game of life is quite important to winning in the game of life. "Important to what?" you ask. Success.

Failure is the most important ingredient for true success and personal and professional growth. Of course, we want to try not to fail, but we shouldn't beat ourselves up if we do. We are human and must try to give ourselves some grace while figuring out how to do life.

What's your latest failure? Was it actually a failure or growth? What did you learn from this failure?

DAY ONE HUNDRED FORTY-SIX

Humans love to stay within our comfort zones because, well
. . . it's the most *comforting* place to us (we think). We don't
want to stretch outside of our comfort zones because it can
cause pain and unwanted anxiety. So, typically, we stay
where we are. We don't make any moves or stretch because
we naturally protect ourselves from that pain or stress.

Comfort zones serve their purpose for us and often protect
us in life. But let's also be clear—no growth is available to us
if we stay within the constraints of our comfort zones. This
is not a suggestion to jump out of your zone in every area
and jolt your nervous system into panic mode, but maybe
when you feel you can trust yourself, take some steps
outside of the zone. It's important for your future. I like to
say, "Your dreams will never meet you in your comfort
zone; rather, they wait for you outside of it." So, go ahead,
be a world changer, step outside, and see what's out there
for yourself.

In what areas of life do you stay in your comfort zone? Why? What would be the worst thing that could happen if you stepped outside?

Day One Hundred Forty-Seven

When it comes to human or material connections, activating your Red Flag Superpower System can save you a lot of time, money, heartache, pain, and stress.

The Red Flag Superpower System (RFSS) is a simple system that recognizes that we all have this superpower; we just aren't aware of it or know how to use it. When caution arises (red flags), this simple system organizes our thoughts and feelings to make more informed decisions.

STOP: *Take a breather.*

EVALUATE: *Find the truth.*

CONCLUDE: *Own the truth.*

ACT: *Proceed or change.*

Red flags aren't always bad, but rather a cautionary sign that we should evaluate whether we will be harmed in a relationship or life event.

What red flags are waving for you right now in your personal or professional life?

DAY ONE HUNDRED FORTY-EIGHT

Coworkers can be amongst the toughest terrain to navigate when it comes to relationships. Some adults cannot handle someone else's talent, skill, or knowledge. They get jealous, talk behind coworkers' backs, downplay the good work of others, or even bully. Can you believe this still happens? As an adult, I continue to self-check how I show up for others and myself.

Coworker relationships are just like any other relationship; we can choose to work on them . . . or not. If some adults cannot handle your success, it's a reflection of them, for the most part. Keep doing your best and moving forward, and don't let someone else's negative vibes kill your good vibes. It's not worth it.

Do you have coworker problems right now? How are you dealing with this? What changes can you make to remedy the issue?

Day One Hundred Forty-Nine

We all know that communication can sometimes seem impossible—even in the best relationships. Humans have complicated brains, emotions, motivations, hormones, and beliefs. It's a miracle we can communicate appropriately at all. Still, communication is one of the most important skills to get right. Communication is the gateway to getting what you want and the most profound connector to other humans.

But communication is a skill. A skill is something we learn and work on. We are not born with communication skills. We learn how to communicate through life experiences and watching our parents/guardians and role models around us. Everyone communicates differently; if we pay attention, we can pick up on how to do it well.

How we communicate is how we are seen, and how we are seen often determines our opportunities.

Are you repeating cycles of communication you learned from family or friends? Does that benefit you or hurt you?

DAY ONE HUNDRED FIFTY

Since we know that we all make mistakes, *how we recover* is the most important part of making those mistakes.

Often, shame takes over when we have messed up, and it is hard to do anything when feeling shame. Shame is so powerful that it's hard to think outside of it. Thankfully, the same thing can happen when we feel gratitude. I always say, "There is not a single emotion that can coexist with gratitude." So, when we mess up, recovery starts with changing the shame to thanks—but the recovery doesn't stop there. We must also change how we do things in order to get a different outcome. You have the power to turn any situation around!

In what area(s) of your life do you feel shame from a mistake? How can you recover by letting go of shame and moving into gratitude?

DAY ONE HUNDRED FIFTY-ONE

Creating healthy boundaries for yourself is one of the greatest forms of self-respect. When we set boundaries with others, we essentially set limits to protect ourselves. We must also set boundaries for ourselves. We can easily hurt ourselves by not setting healthy limits on our own actions and emotions. Boundaries are set for ourselves and others so that everyone knows our limits. When these boundaries are understood clearly, we are proactively limiting unhealthy experiences.

We do have to live and learn what boundaries to set, and this balance can be difficult to figure out, but better late than never, and this learning curve never ends.

What areas can you work on so that your boundaries become clear?

_____

_____

_____

_____

_____

_____

_____

_____

_____

_____

_____

_____

_____

DAY ONE HUNDRED FIFTY-TWO

Believe it or not, there are humans who have genuinely lived a solid and happy life experience despite extreme obstacles, loss, and trauma.

So, how can they say life has been a good experience?

Well, these humans *choose* to have a good experience. They choose to turn the bad into something growth-worthy and life-changing. They choose to keep waking up and doing their best. They choose to take care of themselves and break cycles. They may not always *be* happy, but they *practice* being happy. We can practice happiness in life when we have minimal struggles. Then . . . because we have practiced happiness, when things get more challenging, we don't have to work so hard at convincing ourselves to be happy.

Are you choosing to be happy? If not, what are you choosing and why?

DAY ONE HUNDRED FIFTY-THREE

We were all born good humans with zero hate, jealousy, or greed in our hearts. No human is born with the intent to hurt someone else. When humans appear bad, it's because life hurts them enough to make them want to retaliate. It's our responsibility to recognize this in our human connections.

You were born good, and *you* are still good. Keep doing what you do best, and if there's something that you're not happy with that needs to change, it's a great time to move into transition.

We get what we give.

Is there anything in your life that needs to change for a better life?

DAY ONE HUNDRED FIFTY-FOUR

With the hustle and bustle of life, it's easy to see how we lose ourselves by not realizing our interests or pushing them to the side out of sheer survival mode. We numb our passions and interests because there is little time for them. These are the choices we feel we must make, but what if we could balance necessity and interests? It is possible, but it does require planning, organizing, letting go, and following through.

If we do not feed our souls with our interests and passions, we lose touch with ourselves and the spark of life. Balancing necessities (work) and interests (personal life) will require letting go of some things and following through on others.

Plan

Write a list of things that make your heart smile and feel more excited about life.

Organize

Go through that list and circle two interests/passions most important to you. Write out the time, space, and needs required to bring them to life.

Let Go

There might be other things on your calendar and in life that you need to let go of to incorporate your true interests/passions into your life. It's okay to let go of things not feeding your soul.

Follow Through

Take action steps, and bring these interests into your life, even if it's one interest/passion at a time. You can do this!

DAY ONE HUNDRED FIFTY-FIVE

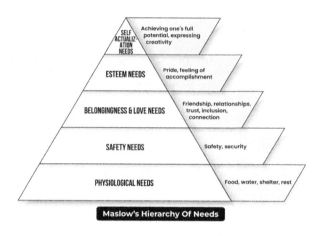

Take a look at Maslow's Hierarchy of Needs[1] pyramid.

We cannot progress up the pyramid to the next stage until the needs for each stage are fulfilled. Our ultimate goal is to be at our full potential most of the time, but each stage has to be fulfilled for that to be experienced. Think about the stages where our youth might be on this pyramid. How can you meet them where they are and help them progress?

[1] Maslow, A. H. (1943). A theory of human motivation. *Psychological Review, 50*(4), 370–396.

Where are you on Maslow's chart for your own development? Where do you feel youth hang out on the chart, and how might you support them as a professional?

DAY ONE HUNDRED FIFTY-SIX

Sometimes, we have to cry . . . and that's okay. Nothing may be wrong, and we still need to cry and release our built-up emotions. Life happens so fast that we push down anything that might get us down in honor of pushing forward.

You are tough, and tears do not make you less tough. Often, tears lead to some sort of revelation, release, or reconciliation, which proves that it's worth letting them flow.

When was the last time you allowed yourself to feel
emotions, tough human?

DAY ONE HUNDRED FIFTY-SEVEN

Laughter is the remedy of all remedies. No medicine on the market can heal us like laughter can. Life is actually funny if we really look around us. Not only is laughter good for us, but when we laugh, it heals other people around us. Life is too short not to laugh and smile as often as we possibly can.

What is your plan today to purposely laugh?

DAY ONE HUNDRED FIFTY-EIGHT

You know how you believe in every student who you teach? How you think they can move mountains if they put their mind to it? How they are brilliant beyond measure? How they embrace the beauty of the world around them? How they have their whole lives ahead of them to do something incredible?

What if you thought the same thing for yourself?

You can move mountains.

You are brilliant beyond measure.

You can embrace the beauty around you.

You have your whole life ahead of you.

You can do something incredible.

Believe in yourself like you believe in others. See what happens.

What are three things you love about yourself today?

DAY ONE HUNDRED FIFTY-NINE

Your resilience this year was stellar. We've covered this in earlier days but it's worth the reminder.

We often think resilience is directly connected to how much we can endure. But the reality is that resilience is the act of repeatedly bouncing back from life events, and each time we bounce back, we become better, understand more, and are stronger. Practicing resilience helps us maintain our passion and interest despite setbacks. The practice of enduring weakens us, and retaining our passion and high work ethic is tough.

When we cultivate resilience rather than heavily enduring life events, we develop higher-functioning coping skills and stress management strategies.

Do you feel you are enduring life events or have learned to be resilient through life events?

DAY ONE HUNDRED SIXTY

Lo and behold, the weight of this school year is starting to lift. Ahhhh . . . yes. You are indeed worthy of a deep breath.

Go ahead, take one.

Think back on how you met new humans this year, supported and encouraged them, and grew as a person and professional because you were in each other's lives.

You have been a rock star for so many people around you. At times, you kept your head up when you wanted to crawl under your desk and sleep. Other times, you cheered on those around you and were their support system because that's what you do—you help others be better versions of themselves.

Well done. It's time to start celebrating for these last twenty days and end this year on a high note.

Whether adult or youth, who did you support this year where you could see that it mattered?

DAY ONE HUNDRED SIXTY-ONE

If there's one thing we know about educators, you are never finished with your job. In the next two weeks, you have opportunities to end this year just how you want. No matter what has happened this year, good or bad, the next two weeks can be magical in organizing, strategizing, and revolutionizing how you will enter your next school year.

If you don't have your own end-of-the-year list going, it might be good to make one and check those items off so you can leave this year with a clear headspace. The better you feel leaving for a break, the better your break will be.

What do you want to do for the next couple of weeks to make you feel like you have done all you can to end this 180-day cycle well?

_____

_____

_____

_____

_____

_____

_____

_____

_____

_____

_____

_____

_____

_____

_____

DAY ONE HUNDRED SIXTY-TWO

Even though educators and students are burned out by this time of year, we have an opportunity to end this school year with gratitude.

There are people you work with, parents, and family who deserve your thanks. If someone made your day, made you feel better, boosted your ego with flattery, or did a great job at something you noticed, write them a note telling them about it and saying thank you.

Educators do not get enough kudos or notices. Be the person who notices and follows through with action on your gratitude thoughts. Your words go a long way toward someone else's well-being.

Who would you like to write a note to in the next week or two and share your thoughts and appreciation?

DAY ONE HUNDRED SIXTY-THREE

Let's face it: our families sometimes suffer because of our careers in education—long hours of grading or extracurricular duties, commitments to other kids, coaching, and less patience at home because of what we manage in a day at work.

It's a good time to stop and enjoy home life even before summer hits. Show appreciation for the tribe at home who supports you. They watch you worry and complain and give your whole heart to your job and those you serve. They have to share you with a lot of people.

Being in the moment with our families is the right thing to do. Even with the end-of-year hustle, it's time to start returning to our home base.

Why are you grateful for your family?

DAY ONE HUNDRED SIXTY-FOUR

The end-of-year cleanout of our spaces is one of the most cathartic practices in education. If you cling to things you no longer need, try shifting your mindset to release the old. With times shifting to digital, do we need to keep so many physical items packed away?

Research shows that clearing out our spaces reduces anxiety, calms our nervous system, and invites clarity into our thinking. Who doesn't want that? It's a free therapy session right there waiting for us.

Enjoy throwing things out! Our mental health is worth it.

Do you love or hate this clearing process at the end of the year? Why?

Day One Hundred Sixty-Five

Integrity until the end. That's what we do as educators. We don't let up, give up, or mess up. Well, we might mess up a little, but we can recover from that. Even if we have hit our planned goals, we still have a big job managing humans, events, and communication at the end of the year. The job doesn't stop because we see the light at the end of the tunnel (a break).

Thank you for your integrity in teaching, keeping everyone safe, and guiding those you serve until the last day.

What does that light at the end of the tunnel look like to you from here?

DAY ONE HUNDRED SIXTY-SIX

One thing is certain at the beginning and end of the school year: we are tired on both ends.

At the beginning of the year, we have to get back in shape; at the end of the year, we are exhausted in body, mind, and spirit. It's like going to the gym daily and jogging for six to eight hours straight while ensuring everyone else is safe, having conversations, teaching, and a hundred other things simultaneously. There's a point where your body, mind, and spirit say, "Okay, I'm done here for a little while."

Congratulations on your well-done juggling act.

What will you do on your first week out of school for the summer?

You know how teachers have the strongest bladders in the world because we never have time to go to the restroom during the day? That's just wild! A basic human need that's not thought about in our profession. What if schools figured out a system where someone traveled to classrooms to allow teachers to run to the restroom at least twice daily? That would be some crazy logic, and any excellent leader who figures that out would dramatically boost their culture's morale.

Soon, you can go to the restroom any time of the day that you want for the summer. That's enough reason to celebrate today!

What else would you like to celebrate today?

Day One Hundred Sixty-Eight

Did you know there are public debates about whether teachers deserve summers off from work?

This is laughable.

Just as parents want to drop their kids off at school for a break, teachers must have a true respite time. We need to re-center, re-focus, and renew ourselves. It's the only way to remain healthy for those we serve.

If you don't have the entire summer off but a break, please embrace every minute and know that you deserve this break and more in life for what you give and share.

Could you stay in the teaching profession year-round without any breaks? Why or why not?

Day One Hundred Sixty-Nine

For whatever it's worth, there are many educators and leaders who have your back. It may not always seem that way, but look around. We are doing this together, and, mostly, we are doing it for the right reasons: to make our world better.

On days when you feel alone, not heard or seen, know that millions of humans in education are getting up in the morning with the same pursuit as you. That's a vast breadth of good energy to hold on to each day.

Have you felt supported, seen, and heard this school year? How?

DAY ONE HUNDRED SEVENTY

With just a few days left, you must feel a range of emotions. As you reflect on the school year, sometimes it's when we finally get in the groove, when we start making real strides, that it comes to an end. This means you have done your job well.

You may feel anxious going into yet another season of unknowns for next year. You may feel apprehensive about a lengthy break and financial responsibilities during this time off of work.

Even when transitions are good, they can still feel stressful and uneasy. When you get to your first day off, you will realize how much you need this for your well-being.

Do you feel stressed or anxious at the end of the school year? Why or why not?

DAY ONE HUNDRED SEVENTY-ONE

Depending on your role in education, your classroom or office is not just a space with desks and chairs. It's a place you created wholeheartedly to make those you serve feel safe, seen, and supported. It's alive and breathing with everyone's energy.

This is no small accomplishment. If parents or others don't say it—thank you for creating a space that ignites growth and creativity, which feeds your students' curiosity and supports their strengths to move forward.

In what ways did you create a space where those around you feel safe, seen, and supported?

DAY ONE HUNDRED SEVENTY-TWO

Keep that smile going for the next few days. Indeed, you may have actually hit the brick wall. You are closing the door and ready to turn in your keys. But keep that smile going for the sake of your mindset and those on your team.

Some of you may be unable to wipe your smile off your face because you are so elated. Know that your positive attitude and energy affect so many in your environment, and we need all the positivity we can get.

In what small ways can you keep the smiles going around you?

_____

_____

_____

_____

_____

_____

_____

_____

_____

_____

_____

_____

_____

_____

DAY ONE HUNDRED SEVENTY-THREE

Maybe this is your first year of teaching, your fifteenth, your thirtieth, or you are retiring. Wherever you are on the career path, know you are appreciated beyond measure. No evaluation can explain what you do or how well you do it.

Hopefully, you find inspiration within each year that leads to a more profound commitment next year, and the next, and the next . . .

What has inspired you this year to continue sharing your skills and talents and committing to education?

DAY ONE HUNDRED SEVENTY-FOUR

Looking back on this year, there were many growth areas for those you serve and yourself. These growth areas make your heart happy, which is why you stay in this profession.

You were part of that growth, whether it was student achievement or social-skill maturity. For you, many things contribute to your happiness: positive relationships, professional development, the opportunity to have autonomy in what you do, or success in work-life balance.

Whatever the reason for happiness, notice it for what it is, and don't let it get clouded by exhaustion or procedures. Happiness is hard to come by; embrace what you have created.

What made your heart the happiest this past year?

DAY ONE HUNDRED SEVENTY-FIVE

Sure, some things will change for next school year because that's what is constant in education. Try to be careful of where you put your energy in the changes. Some changes that are asked of us are illogical, not worth the time to worry about, and some are detrimental. Some changes are incredibly positive and good. Find balance in how you can make the most of changes, whether advocating for something else or celebrating the good.

We can't control everything, but we do have a voice. Let's use it in an integrity-driven way. You got this!

What changes do you know are coming your way next year? What do you want to let go of, fight, or find peace with?

DAY ONE HUNDRED SEVENTY-SIX

You can start celebrating—if you haven't already.

But while you celebrate, applaud yourself for knocking this year out of the park! Whether you had a tough year or the best year of your career, you win either way because you didn't just make it; you changed lives, cared for others and yourself, and made it to home plate with your arms wide open.

Now you deserve a rest.

What are a few things you did this year that deserve a celebration?

Day One Hundred Seventy-Seven

Finding hobbies, interests, and passions outside of our profession is imperative to internal wealth. Beyond external achievements or material possessions, the abundance we experience within ourselves is our internal wealth. This wealth can comprise everything we covered in these 180 days: gratitude, self-acceptance, resilience, purpose, mindfulness, compassion, talents, emotional intelligence, and more.

During your break, intentionally grow your internal wealth however you can.

How can you grow your internal wealth? It could be through activities like reading a book, learning a new skill, spending time with loved ones, or engaging in a hobby. The key is to invest in activities that bring you joy and fulfillment.

Day One Hundred Seventy-Eight

One student at a time, one peer teacher at a time, one faculty/staff member at a time, one team member at a time—you are making a difference. Your unwavering commitment to your profession makes our world a better place.

Thank you for your compassion, understanding, forgiveness, advocacy, and love.

It's an honor to work with you.

Who made your job easier this year so you could share your gifts and give like you did?

Want to thank them?

_____

_____

_____

_____

_____

_____

_____

_____

_____

_____

_____

_____

_____

_____

_____

_____

DAY ONE HUNDRED SEVENTY-NINE

It's bittersweet, right? A little natural smile is returning, but anxiety accompanies closing out a school year. Our work is never done. But we should get to a good stopping place and pause things until next year. We can think about what we want to change or do better for next year, but there is no need to keep working over the summer if you don't have to. Space and time between years are purposeful because we must recharge and reset our intentions. That's how heavy our work can be.

Since you have given everything you have to your job this year, start shifting to the mindset of "self-renewal."

What are ways you plan to renew yourself this summer?

DAY ONE HUNDRED EIGHTY

Look at you; you've made it! Despite how slow the days felt along the way, it's now apparent how swiftly the year has passed. I commend you for your perseverance, showing up, leaving your mark, and transforming lives. Your contributions have once again served the greater good-our future.

It's crucial that you prioritize self-care and indulge in activities you love this summer. This break is not just a luxury; it's a necessity for rejuvenating our minds, nurturing our bodies, pursuing our passions, and resting. You can take care of yourself by looking at life from multiple perspectives.

You have done well. You may never know your influence, but you can bet that it will infuse future generations with the same dedication and passion you've shown.

Take a moment to reflect on this past school year. In what areas did you improve professionally and personally? In what areas are you still learning and growing? How did your perspective change this year?

About the Author

Living a multi-hyphenate lifestyle, J.D. Durden is a dedicated teacher, culture consultant, author, and songwriter. With several Teacher of the Year awards on her shelf, she is unapologetically committed to a human-first philosophy within education, balancing her life as a wife, mom, and aunt—while living creatively. As a songwriter, her graduation songs are among the most played/streamed songs for graduations worldwide. She intensely studies environments, sets off ripples of change, plants seeds of hope, and is a pretty good kid's lunch maker and fixer of random things.

J.D. Durden founded Education Renovation, a consulting and publishing company. E.R.'s mission is to "Keep what works, improve what doesn't" in each unique school environment. E.R. guides a roadmap for school leaders and teacher teams to be the ultimate project managers in repairing, renewing, and rebuilding their dream schools.

J.D. Durden has a degree in English Literature, a Master's in Business Administration and Project Management, and is Certified in Leadership Innovation.

Made in the USA
Columbia, SC
29 September 2024

43259914R00205